From Consulting to Cutting

Memoirs of a Hair Salon Owner

NICOLE BARRETT

NyreePress

From Consulting to Cutting: Memoirs of a Hair Salon Owner
Published by NyreePress Literary Group
P.O. Box 164882
Fort Worth, TX 76161
Order copies in bulk by calling 972-793-3736 or request a quote by sending an email to info@nyreepress.com.
www.nyreepress.com
Dallas, Texas

ISBN print 978-0-9910489-8-4
ISBN ebook 978-0-9903486-3-4

Autobiography / Business / Inspirational

Copyright © 2010, 2014 by Nicole Barrett. All rights reserved. No portion of this book may be reproduced in any form without the written permission of the copyright owner, except for brief excerpts quoted in critical reviews.

Printed in the United States of America

Endorsements

For the career-oriented Cosmetologist, this literature is a must read. In this field, there is a distinct dichotomy: Stylists who treat this Industry as it is a hobby for them, and Stylists who have made hairdressing their profession. By being goal-oriented, business savvy, and focused, Nicole's memoir proves that she has made this occupation her profession. This book is complexed with simplicity. The complexity is in Nicole's consistency and steadfastness. The simplicity lies in the fact that she just did it. Whatever needed to be done. No excuses, only results. Nicole has outlined a seamless guide to salon success for both stylists and proprietors. Nicole's business ethic is so disciplined, that it transcends salon walls. Anyone in any profession can apply her formula, and reap the reward of success.

Tay Myrie
Master Cosmetologist/Salon Manager

From Consulting to Cutting is a cutting-edge reality check that proves you can be just as successful in the world of entrepreneurship, as you can be in corporate America. This book is truly motivating for anyone, but especially for those who have the deep desire to be bold and step out on faith. A lot of faith mixed with work ethic will take you to places you can't even dream of yet. This book is just the kick you need to get you up and going. As a successful owner of an Atlanta-based law firm, I have been re-inspired to work harder, take leaps of faith and dare to dream big. I promise you this book will do the same for you regardless of your passion in life.

Joi R. Fairell, Esq.

Contents

INTRODUCTION	8
BUSINESS PARTNERS	11
FINDING A MENTOR	18
STARTING OUT AS AN ASSISTANT	24
EDUCATION AND EXPERIENCE	28
KEEP YOUR FOCUS ON THE VISION	33
DEALING WITH ADVERSITY	38
SERVITUDE IS GRATITUDE	42

From Consulting to Cutting

Memoirs of a Hair Salon Owner

NICOLE BARRETT

Dedication

For my mom, Beverly. I've learned so many lessons from you. Through all of the years, all of the periods of growth and celebration, you have never left my side and I love you more than life. To my brothers Troy and Marcus, Thank you; you always believed in me and never gave up on me. To my beautiful daughter Gabriella, thank you for coming into my life at the right time and teaching me what true love, patience, and prosperity really are. To Nia, for sharing in my youth with me and for helping me to become the woman that I am today. To Wilecia, Keshon, LaMonica and Ricky, thank you for teaching me what true friendship is. To all of my friends and family who have lived my testimony with me. And to an entire creed of Entrepreneurs and those wanting to become one, this is for you.

What it takes to be number one

1. A contagious positive attitude
2. To be excited at the prospect of helping others
3. To be self-assured, not arrogant
4. To like people, and get them to like you
5. Not just book smart, street smart
6. If you're not having fun, whats the point
7. Do everything full force
8. Unspoken integrity, visible honesty...If you have to say you are, then you're probably not
9. Concentrate on the details without getting caught up in them
10. Be kid-like happy on the inside

~Jeffery Gitomer

Introduction

THERE ARE SO MANY THINGS THAT I could write about. So many stories, so many life lessons, so many failures, mistakes, and so many great people that I have met along the way. And as I write, I'm trying to think: In what direction do I want to take this book? How personal is *too personal*? What story do I *really* want to tell? A personal one, a business one, or both? As these thoughts race back and forth through my mind, I decide to start writing anyway and whatever comes out will come to life.

As long as I can remember, I've always loved to write. Since I was eight years old, I have always written in a journal. I loved capturing thoughts, capturing moments, capturing dreams, and creating the blueprint for my future. When I would go back to read what I had already written, I felt as if I was reliving my life all over again. So it came as no surprise that in my young adult life, I wanted to start a business. Earlier on, I had identified that I loved creating things from the ground up, and maintaining those things for years to come, no matter the struggle that came with it.

So gradually my writing started as ideas in my mind, to thoughts on paper, to manifestations of a real-life business, and that was so dope to me, because I would read about rags-to-riches stories, but I never thought that I would live one. See, to me, "riches" doesn't always have to present itself in the form of money. Riches can be prosperity. A wise man once said that true prosperity is when nothing is missing and nothing is broken in your life. I work so hard at finding that balance. And it was in finding that balance that I actually found myself and my business. Here's my testimony...

"The critical ingredient is getting off your butt and doing something. It's as simple as that. A lot of people have ideas, but there are few who decide to do something about them now. Not tomorrow. Not next week. But today. The true Entrepreneur is a doer, not a dreamer."

~ **Nolan Bushnell**

ONE

Business Partners

WHEN I FIRST MET NIA, I WAS fresh out of college and starting my career at a Human Resources outsourcing firm. I remember setting up my cubicle with family pictures, books like *Who Moved my Cheese?*, and tons of pens and pencils stationed neatly on my desktop. She sat in the cubicle next to mine. One day I went to lunch with her and her friend. And from that point on, Nia and I started a friendship that would last for years. We both shared our dreams of entrepreneurship: She wanted to start a hair salon, and I wanted to start a mentoring program.

We toyed around with the idea of being business partners, but before we delved into business, we decided to build trust amongst each other. We agreed to put some money up, just to see where our heads were at, and to prove to one another that we would make the investment (even though it felt much more like a sacrifice). Saving is a disciplinary action that both young and old should conform to, or at least attempt to conform to. With that being said, we decided to invest $500 apiece in the stock market. At the time that was a lot of money to us - and what was so crazy about it was that we lost all of that money due to choosing bad investments. But you live and you learn. Shortly thereafter, Nia was presented with a new job opportunity at a consulting firm. Four months later, she got me a job there too. It was at our new company where we put our minds to work and started really going hard on the thought of starting a business.

    I remember being so excited about the fact that I had finally met someone who was so much like me. We were so fearless, so naive, yet so dedicated. Over time we became really good friends, and as our friendship blossomed, so did the business plan for our hair salon. Neither of us came from an elite social class, but we did come from a background that emphasized love, education, self-worth, being passionate about your dreams, confidence, determination, hard-work, and drive. We were the perfect match.

* * *

In 2006, we really laid the framework for what we wanted to do. We started narrowing down the services industry: We researched the hotel industry, but realized that it wasn't our niche. We considered working in the construction field, however we deemed ourselves unfit at the time. We tried our hand at real estate, but we weren't as lucky as others who were flipping houses and profiting. But when we researched the hair industry, we were so intrigued. Here was an industry that, at one point in time, was highly valued. Your hairdresser and/or barber was *highly* revered in his/her community. The shop/salon was a place where folk congregated and conversed about current events.

As we researched the people that pioneered the hair industry, we took a liking to Madam C.J. Walker, and Alonzo Herndon. Here were two visionaries that defied all odds and took a business approach to the beauty industry. Both were self-made millionaires. Madam C.J. Walker created a line of hair products and was the first black female millionaire. Alonzo

Herndon owned the famed "Crystal Palace," a barbershop in Atlanta that was located on Peachtree Street, and he later founded the Atlanta Life Insurance Company. Nia and I believed that we could come into the beauty industry and make a greater impact on the African-American community by servicing clients, and serving the community by stimulating jobs and making a positive impact on society as a whole. So we knew that it was time to hustle.

We put ourselves on a budget. For two years straight we ate rice and gravy for lunch every day, and sometimes we would switch it up and eat a wheat bun with lettuce, tomato, cheese, and pickles. Everyone thought we were nuts, but little did they know spending less than $2.00 on lunch every day was setting us up on our path to success. We were always traveling for our job, so while in different states, we would do more research on our downtime, and have conference calls about what we learned, what research we did, and what our goals would be for the month, etc. On Fridays, we would meet up in our office and go full throttle—no brakes—on our road to starting our business. Once we got our ideas on paper, we knew that it was time to find some mentors.

We researched the best black hair salons in Georgia, picked our top ten, and made arrangements to contact and meet each of the salon owners. We were so ready, so green, and we just knew that these salon owners would love to share their success stories with us and help us. Little did we know that we would be so disappointed.

One thing that we had to understand was that we had to be truthful to ourselves, our vision, and our goals. We quickly realized that everyone didn't believe in our vision, and we learned that in life, there are no handouts. We walked away disappointed from countless lunch meetings with these salon owners.

We were so confused. We questioned ourselves over and over again. Did no one want to help us? Were we coming off the wrong way? It seemed like every door of opportunity that presented itself was closed. But we refused to let anyone cloud our vision and ruin our dreams, so we kept it moving. We enrolled in beauty school, because we knew that in order for others to take us seriously as owners, we would have to invest in ourselves. We would travel for work Monday thru Thursday, and go to school Thursday evenings, and all day on Fridays and Saturdays. On Sundays we would try to spend time with our boyfriends at the time, and then prepare to do it all again the following week. It took us two years to finish. I remember it feeling like the longest two years of my life. So from 2005-2010, we literally spent six days a week together—every waking moment of every day together working on the business. We lived, ate, and breathed building the salon. That was solely our major focus. And we were truly focused.

"Whatever you do, you need courage. Whatever course you decide upon, there is always someone to tell you that you are wrong. There are always difficulties arising that tempt you to believe your critics are right. To map out a course of action and follow it to an end requires some of the same courage that a soldier needs. Peace has its victories, but it takes brave men and women to win them."

~ Ralph Waldo Emerson

Two

Finding a Mentor

WE WANTED TO IDENTIFY ourselves with someone in whom we could look up to, whose values modeled our values, someone who was ethical and honest, and an all-around good person. So we researched, and originally we narrowed our search for a mentor to someone who was in the salon industry as an owner, and someone whom we felt that we could identify ourselves with on a personal and professional level. I remember us being so excited—we thought everyone was so nice, and that everyone could relate to where we were coming from and where we were going. But like I said earlier, that was not the case. We had a hard time in the beginning. There were many doors that were closed to us, a lot of people were skeptical of us, thinking that we wanted their information, or something from them, and then some people were just not responsive to us, because they felt they had to work hard to get to the top, so we would have to as well. Now there is nothing wrong with that, because we valued hard work; however, when it comes to "entitlement" issues, we believe that we all can work with and leverage off one another. So my point is that we had to come to the conclusion that not everyone is nice, not everyone wanted to help or share information, and not everyone wanted to see us succeed. We regrouped, we sat down, and we decided to broaden our search for a mentor by looking for an individual who was in the seven-figure income bracket. We went for it.

We did our research and came up with five owners who we would have liked to meet. Consequently, we had Brian, owner of a prominent salon in Gwinnett County, on both of our lists, so we agreed to reach out to him. One day while at lunch, we called the number to his corporate office. His secretary answered, but was hesitant to put us in direct contact with him, so she sent our call to his voicemail. We decided not to leave a message, and hung up. We were frustrated, but then Nia said, "just call him again right now, something is telling me that you should." So I dialed the number again, and to our surprise, he picked up on the first ring! The conversation went something like this:

"Hello. I know this is weird, but my name is Nicole, and my friend's name is Nia, and we did some research on you and know all about you. We would really like to meet you."

"Ooooookkkkkkkkkkk," he replied.

"And we believe in entrepreneurship and philanthropy and we love what you stand for."

"Well, thank you so much," he said. "I would love to meet you both as well."

And from there, we spent a good year meeting with Brian, getting to know him and him getting to know us. It wasn't until a year and a half later that we even presented the idea of an upscale salon for the African-American community.

I remember we met in his office, we had our "value proposition" in PowerPoint, we were so confident and so sure that he would partner with us. After presenting everything to him, we asked him to be our business partner. He never answered us, but told us that he would be in touch. We were devastated! How could he turn us down? Was he not sold on the vision? A week later, he called us to come back to his office. I will never forget what he said:

> *"Owning a business is difficult. You have to really want it. You have to want it with a passion. It took me several years to get to the point that I am today. There was a lot of sacrifice involved, and a lot of sweat and tears. I'm proud of you girls, but I want you to understand that when what you do during the times that you are planning your business supersedes what you do on your 9-5. You have to ask yourselves if you are at the point in which you want to make your business your main priority."*

He left us with that. So we went back to work, we sat and planned and thought and cried and planned again. We knew that we wanted to start our business, but what if it didn't work out? We already had a hard time getting our peers to accept the fact that we wanted to leave a comfortable job to own a salon. So we really put much thought into it, prayed, and did what we had to do. We called Brian seven days later and told him that we had quit our jobs as consultants, and were now salon assistants at the best black hair care salon in Atlanta. And not only were we starting as assistants, we had arranged to study under top stylists in both New York City and Chicago. Brian was sold. In life, sometimes you just have to take the risk, even if it seems like the odds are stacked up against you. Time passed and we pressed on. We eventually graduated from beauty school.

We remained assistants - no one saw us as a threat, so we quickly learned what to do and what not to do in the salon business. We planned, and worked, and planned. Ironically we had the hardest time trying to figure out what to name our salon. We wanted something meaningful, so we stuck both of our names together and named the salon NiaNicole Salon. It's so crazy, because once we got the ball rolling on planning and unveiling our salon, a lot of the people that originally turned us down when we had reached out for mentoring, now wanted to talk and meet with us.

"I had to make my own living and my own opportunity! But I made it! Don't sit down and wait for the opportunities to come. Get up and make them!"

~ Madam C.J. Walker

Three

Starting out as an Assistant

BEING AN ASSISTANT GOES DOWN IN my life as one of the most humbling experiences—hands down. I say that because you have to understand that there is an ego (unknowingly, sometimes) that comes with working for a consulting firm. So Nia and I went through a drastic change. We were young, we were traveling, we had rental cars, credit cards...we pretty much were living what we thought was the American dream. And when we made the decision to quit our jobs, it was a hard pill to swallow; not just for other people—but for us as well. We literally went from consulting to cutting: From sitting in the offices of high-powered executives to cleaning bathrooms and washing hair. But when I look back, the decision that we made was so dope because I'm not sure if the average person would have done what we did. Mentally, we had to literally re-train our minds. So we did. And we worked hard. I mean *super-hard*. Fortunately, we both worked at the same salon, and at the time, it was the best black hair care salon in Atlanta.

It was crazy because I would oftentimes see former co-workers come into the salon. They would look at me like, "Wow, she fell off." Nia and I kept our dream a secret, so when former co-workers or other people that we knew came into the salon to be serviced, we just told them that we wanted to switch gears a little bit. Hilarious!

Every day we worked, we went home and took notes. We learned the technical aspect of hair, we learned how to provide great customer service, we learned how to deal with conflict resolution, and we learned how to run a business. Like I stated earlier, no one saw us as a threat.

There were so many days that we did not want to go to work. We were so tired! And besides that, we were still saving and planning, and trying to have some sort of personal life. My boyfriend at the time ended up cheating on me. I guess I should have paid him more attention, or maybe he should have waited. Who knows. All I know is that I was on my dustle (I doubled my hustle), on my grind. In the summer of 2007, Nia went to New York City and shadowed a top stylist, and I went to Chicago to study under one as well. I'm telling you, we learned more in that year than we ever thought that we would. We worked as assistants for almost a year before we became stylists.

"Experience taught me a few things. One is to listen to your gut, no matter how good something sounds on paper. The second is that you're generally better off sticking with what you know. And the third is that sometimes your best investments are the ones you don't make."

~ **Donald Trump**

Four

Education and Experience

I WENT TO THE UNIVERSITY OF Georgia, and graduated with a degree in Business. I worked for great companies. I was blessed to have had the opportunity to travel and work for different companies, and I met great people along the way. About three years into my profession, I went to beauty school to obtain my license to do hair, so on paper, I was very accomplished. I am extremely grateful and blessed to have had the opportunity to obtain a great education, but truth be told, NONE of this trumps the experience that I gained. Because there is nothing like learning as you go, outside of a formal and structured education.

Some of the best lessons learned in my life were learned as I lived. After four years of college, nothing prepared me for the workforce more than learning on the job. Granted, I learned from school and from my educators how to talk "the talk," personal and professional etiquette, and how to handle myself accordingly, but it wasn't until I started working that I learned the unwritten rules. Because a major challenge for me was that, as a black female, I felt as if I had to work three times as hard as my peers to gain the same accolades and acceptance. While I was working in consulting, I had been planning away and working on the foundation of the salon. Towards the end of my career in consulting, I took a trip to St. Kitts and Nevis. While there, I stayed in a time-share, and during the time-share presentation, I met a man that I will never forget.

He had completed his time-share presentations for the day, so we had a great conversation about everything—in general. He told me that he was born in London, but resided in the United States while working in the hoteling industry. During his time in the US, he had an opportunity to move overseas and expand that aspect of the Industry that he was in. While in St. Kitts, he managed to start his own business on the side, and was preparing to leave the company that he was working for to dedicate himself to his business 100 percent. He gave me great advice and insight into how this could be done, with hard work and preparation. I told him part of my plan, and how I was going about it. He left me with a quote that said, "Luck is when preparation meets the opportunity," and he gave me a book titled *The Richest Man In Babylon*. I still have that book today. He wished me luck, and said that one day, we may run into each other again, somewhere in the world.

I came back to the United States refreshed and energized, ready to hit the ground running. One of the first stops Nia and I made was the bank, so that we could obtain a business loan. We were so excited: We had $22,500 in cash, three properties between the two of us, and great credit scores. But we were told by the banker that they were unable to approve us for a loan because there had been no successful African-American salons that had set the precedent. We were crushed. Needless to say, a lot of what we did in the building phases of our salon came from our own money. No loans. We opened NiaNicole Salon October 27, 2008, which was later said to be one of the toughest days on Wall Street. But we did our best with what we had, studied the market, studied our competition, and saw this experience as an opportunity to prove ourselves to ourselves. And when we opened our doors, we may not have had any clients, but while other businesses were closing, we decided to attract their clients by offering free services to build our clientele. This, in turn, boosted consumer confidence while promoting our business. While most businesses were trying to figure out how they were going to stay afloat in a tough economy, we were ready to figure out how we were going to gain their clientele. This experience taught us that working for free helps you to not build a dependency on money alone. And as a result, we were able to gain the competitive advantage.

"One reason so few of us achieve what we truly want is that we never direct our focus; we never concentrate our power. Most people dabble their way through life, never deciding to master anything in particular."

~ **Tony Robbins**

FIVE

Keep Your Focus on the Vision

It was the spring of 2006, and Nia and I decided that we would like to produce an additional stream of income that would be used to help fund our salon. During this time, the housing market was booming. There were tons of reality shows showing investors buying houses, renovating them, putting them back on the market within an extremely short period of time, and then selling them for a profit. It looked so easy and so promising, so we decided that we would try it for ourselves. Both of us had already owned homes, and since these investment properties that we would be interested in buying wouldn't be our primary residences, we didn't see it as a big risk. We just knew that we could flip a property in three months. One of our mentors was a realtor, so we utilized her knowledge and her services.

Although our realtor explained to us the opportunities and vulnerabilities of owning multiple properties and the difficulty in maintaining them; we didn't see our decision to invest in the market as a huge risk. So we justified our decision. Property hunting, here we go. Within two months of searching, we found the property of our dreams. It had five bedrooms, four bathrooms, a finished basement, and a huge front and back yard. It was in a well-established neighborhood, and a good school zone. The asking price was $141,000; we put less than $5,000 down. We quickly rushed in to this purchase, even when the home inspection revealed that there had been a flood in the basement.

After literally two months of owning and renovating this property, there was a bad storm in the area and the basement flooded. This cut into our budget, and we found ourselves taking money away from the salon in order to maintain this property. Once we renovated it and fixed it up real nice and pretty, it flooded again! We had to invest more money into replacing the carpet, water heater, etc. We had numerous insurance claims, and lots of headaches. Shortly thereafter we put it on the market.

We had a few interested buyers, but none who were serious enough to purchase, due to the floods in the basement. Our dream of flipping within three months was no longer a reality. We saw how careful others were in doing their research, and we resentfully wished that we had done the same. So we took it off the market and began to look for a renter, being that we had paid our second month's mortgage on that property It was becoming a real financial burden. We easily found tenants, but then the tenants would have tons of complaints about the property, and we felt bad because we could not financially afford to address all of their needs.

Then the worst happened. Our tenant abandoned the house after a while. We were left with a *huge* mortgage that we could not afford. We had no choice but to try and short-sale the property. But that didn't work. Our property then went into foreclosure, and our credit rating was hit big time. Huge lesson learned. After the dust settled, we realized that we had lost over $35,000 on that property— money that could have been used for building our salon.

One of the biggest lessons that I have ever learned is that focus is a blend of intention, discipline, and skill. We found ourselves working on many time-consuming tasks at any given time. We learned that it took away that discipline from our primary goal (which was building the salon), and spread it out amongst many goals.

"A leader must lead. Where others see obstacles, he must see opportunities. When others see problems, he must see possibilities. Civilization is not built on a negation, but on an affirmation— an affirmation of the bright and promising possibilities that the future holds for those who are enterprising enough to pursue them."

~ David J. Vaughan

Six

Dealing with Adversity, while Starting Your Business

IMAGINE FOLLOWING YOUR DREAM, and then giving it all up: the money, the prestige, the career. Then imagine things going south. Completely. Things were going great for us at first, because we had our arms around everything. Nia and I were managing our personal properties efficiently, we had money saved in the bank, we were planning, meeting, volunteering, and both of us were in serious relationships. Let's just say it seems as if when one bad thing happens, everything else follows suit.

I remember a time when I had no money; gas was $4.05 a gallon and I had no gas in my tank. I lost my debit card, and went through a breakup, all in the same day. I remember that day clearly: It was raining, and I was so sad, I remember walking in the rain, calling my older brother to come and get me, because I was so depressed. It was my younger brother's birthday, and I could hardly pull myself together to finally call him to say happy birthday. I didn't want him to know that I was sad, because my family worried about me so much. I went through so much pain, and that was one of the toughest points in my life.

One day a few weeks after all of that happened, I looked in the mirror, and didn't even know who I was, because I was twenty pounds thinner, and could barely fit my clothes. Then I remember thinking to myself, "I give up." I felt as if I couldn't take it anymore. I really prayed those days and nights, and my family and friends helped to keep me going. So I started to set deadlines, and since I felt as if life was too much, I decided to take it a day at a time. I started getting back on track with my goals, and really focusing all of my positive energies on studying for my hair exam which was coming up in a few weeks, and building my clientele. Everything had been restored in my life, but better than it ever was before.

My mom always says that nothing good in life comes easy. That statement could not be truer. Now, when I think of adversity, I think of this: I think of a plant that I can buy from a store. The pot that the plant has been placed in is too small. So I buy a bigger pot for the plant, and I buy more dirt to fill the big pot. Then I uproot the plant from the original pot - and in the process I may have cut off some roots, maybe left some dirt in the old pot. I've now placed the plant into the larger pot, and mixed in the new dirt with the old dirt. Then I water it, and after a while, the plant grows larger than it ever could have in its old pot.

They say that as much as you are willing to give up is exactly how much God is willing to put in your life. So Nia and I gave it all up. And it was worth it.

"Everybody can be great...because anybody can serve....You only need a heart full of grace...."

~ Martin Luther King Jr.

Seven

Servitude is Gratitude

When I worked in consulting, I had heard of a gentleman who was on a certain project. He was a senior manager, and had a high rank in the company. He had worked himself so hard, that he had a heart attack right there on the client's site. He was rushed to the hospital, and to everyone's surprise, he was back at work the next day, because he said that he wanted to fully dedicate himself to his work and nothing else. He didn't even give himself time to heal! At that point in time, I thought to myself the importance of a professional career, but also the importance of taking a step back sometimes and appreciating life, because at any moment, you could lose it.

There is a certain thing called gratitude. Gratitude is thankfulness, an appreciation, a state of being thankful for the things and the people that we have in our lives. And sometimes, just sometimes, it takes a person being in gratitude to enjoy the journey. That gentleman who had the heart attack and went to work the next day has always stuck with me in the back of my mind, because I was the type of person who could work myself to death, *literally*. When I was pregnant, I worked up until three days before my daughter was born. I had a cesarean, and three weeks after giving birth, I went back to work. I was no better than that guy who went back to work after a heart attack. Because my motto at the time was, "Grind day is from Friday to Friday." I did understand that when you are in the process of starting and running a small business, it is easy to neglect yourself, and your loved ones, because your definition of success, at that time, is seeing the company grow, and seeing profits. But oftentimes, you have to realize that your health comes first.

Early in life, I recognized that the more I gave, the more I received. Each year, during the early stages of NiaNicole Salon, Nia and I chose three organizations to contribute to financially, as well as donate our time and our hands. I've carried on this tradition. For me, it's just something about knowing that I've contributed to making that difference in someone's life. There is an old saying that states, "If you bless the lives of the people around you, then they will turn around and make your name great." I truly believe that. Most of the greatest moments in my life came when I gave—gave money, gave time, and gave birth.

So in my early thirties, I learned to enjoy the journey. I can say that I've had my fair share of experiences. I've had seasons of love, pain, departure, restoration, and the list goes on and on. But through it all, I've learned that these have all been seasons of growth and change. Some seasons were meant to propel me into a new phase in life, others were meant to slow me down. But during those really trying storms, I learned to depend on God for wisdom and direction.

Although I'm humbled and proud to say that I've made it to my sixth year in business, I'm also a living testament that no matter what you may go through, if you just stick it out, if you put 10,000 hours in, and if you allow your mistakes to be your mentors and your guides, then you will always hold your posture, and you will always find success. There's no way around it. Because putting in that sweat equity speaks volumes to your character and your ability of being above-average; and as we all know, average people aren't sitting at the tables where decisions are being made.

NYREEPRESS LITERARY GROUP
"PUBLISHING LIFE FOR FAMILIES"
WWW.NYREEPRESS.COM
WWW.BUGLOVEBOOKS.COM
TWITTER: @NYREEPRESS

www.ingramcontent.com/pod-product-compliance
Lightning Source LLC
Chambersburg PA
CBHW062243300426
44110CB00034B/1915